Look at This Tree! What Do You See?

Text and photos by Maggy Bruzelius

Look at This Tree! What Do You See?

Text and photography copyright © 2019 by Maggy Bruzelius

Cover design by Trina Baker (http://catriona-baker-69uj.squarespace.com)

Book design by Sarah E. Holroyd (https://sleepingcatbooks.com)

brusospublishing@gmail.com

ISBN 978-0-578-43620-3
Library of Congress Control Number: 2019902883

Summary: When children look carefully at the photos of these trees they will find surprises! They will be able to imagine all sorts of animal faces and will want to go outside to look at more trees.

Subjects: Nature, trees: nonfiction; Look, observe, go outside, find tree faces: nonfiction.

Acknowledgments: Special thanks to Trina Baker who helped me enormously with her design skills! Many thanks to April Price, Sarah Goodman, Laura Wainwright, Morgan Baker, Nancy DuVergne Smith, Kate Feiffer, Clara Flender, Greta Flender, Margaret Howard, Catherine Martin, Heather Shaw, Happy Sponberg and Steve Sponberg. Their advice, help, and support have been invaluable.

For Emilie, Joli, and John
whose constant encouragement
and humor made this book happen.

Looking at trees

takes a knack.

Look really close.

Then stand back.

You might find
what you least expect.
You'll be glad
you looked and checked.

Look at this tree!

What do you see?

Is that a branch

reaching towards us?

Or maybe...

A snake making a fuss?

Look at this tree!

What do you see?

Do you see a dry,

leafless limb?

Or maybe . . .

An alligator, out for a swim?

Look at this tree!

What do you see?

Could this be a trunk,
where bark fell away?

Or perhaps . . .

A face, hoping to play?

Look at this tree!

What do you see?

Is this a low hanging

tree limb

facing the sun?

Or maybe...

A dog sitting after a run?

Look at this tree!

What do you see?

Is this a tree trunk
rotting right there?

Or perhaps...

A face mask ready to wear?

Look at this tree!

What do you see?

Is this a broken down tree
with a vine out of place?

Or perhaps...

A giraffe standing tall
hiding its face?

Look at this tree!

What do you see?

Is this a tree trunk with lots
of curves and bumps?

Or maybe...

An old man

down in the dumps?

Look at this tree!

What do you see?

Is this just the top limb
of an old tree?

Or is there...

A bird?

What does it see?

Look at this tree!

What do you see?

Is this a m-m-monster,
roaring with rage?

Or maybe...

It's singing on a monster stage?

Look at this tree!

What do you see?

Shhhh! Look closely, but...

be aware.

Try not to wake up the sweet

sleeping bear!

Look at this tree!

What do you see?

A tree trunk with insects
and woodpecker bores?

Or perhaps...

A laughing face

looking at yours?

What might cause
this hidden face?

A broken branch,
a twisted place,

A patch of bark,
a growth, some scrapes?

Some trees grow in funny shapes.

The next time you get close
to a tree,
Look for the things that only
you can see.

And remember...

Looking at trees
takes a knack.
Look really close and
then stand back!

Author's Note

I decided to write this book because I love trees and I would like young children to enjoy them as much as I do! Trees are very mysterious to me because there are so many hereditary and environmental factors that effect their growth and health. I don't think any two trees are exactly identical.

You can see that storms, insects, different kinds of soil, and changes in temperature effect trees in different ways. And these things are only just a few of the environmental factors that change trees.

It is very easy to see how prevailing winds can cause trees to grow in one direction. You can also see how other wind disturbances coupled with rain and different soils can cause snapped tree trunks and deformed canopies. The list of factors and effects goes on and on.

Why any particular tree looks the way it does is difficult to ascertain, if not impossible! That for me is why observing trees is so interesting. You can see differences when you walk the same trail day after day because natural processes are constantly working and interacting causing small and big changes.

I hope this book encourages readers to appreciate trees the way I do!